Conversation about Withering

Cristina Sánchez López

&

Aryanil Mukherjee

Moria Books -- Chicago -- 2020

copyright © 2020 Cristina Sánchez López &
Aryanil Mukherjee

ISBN: 978-1-7337148-3-9

cover art   Mario Agudelo Jaramillo

book design   William Allegrezza

moria c/o William Allegrezza
1151 E. 56th #2 Chicago, IL 60637
http://www.moriapoetry.com

Table of Contents

Prolusion   4

A liturgy of encounter   5
awaits us at the threshold

Where foundations lay   17
of forgotten bridges

The pulp torments,   27
inside unspent juices churn

As osmosis demonstrates   46
this invisible dye of pain

Prolusion

In the spring of 2015, a chance poetic conversation began between two poets separated by decades, continents, languages and literary traditions. Colombian poet Cristina Sánchez López was writing from her bed, irreversibly ailed by aortic aneurysm and congestive heart failure leading to multiple complications. With reduced mobility, "breathing room" and daily bouts of bleeding and excruciating pain, Cristina was living a vestige of a life hanging like icicle from a sliver of desperate hope. Writing, when her body permitted, became her mechanism of deconstruction. Almost all of her bedridden work assumed an epistolary form and was directed at Aryanil Mukherjee, a bilingual Indian American poet whose work she had found on the web and began to admire. In response to her poetic inquiry, Aryanil began advancing the conversation in the form of a poem, taking it to crevices of comfort extrinsic to both the plexus of pain and the refuge of nature. A part of this ongoing conversation, conducted in its entirety via texting makes the content of this book.

A liturgy of encounter

awaits us at the threshold

Mon, May 11, 7:32 pm

Dear A,

Life is the sum total of instants
it exploits and what we know about it
depends upon constrictions
of intentionality.

On the scales of feelings, reality rises
as an immigrated object from the margins
of our acceptance.

On the stream of days and nights,
it is the passing of all that pushes us to its limits,
making us only float like
butterflies.

Experience brings with it an
unending disorder of time, but
the instants project
a luxurious suggestion: movement.

Now, what is living, but tolerating
the heterogeneity of themes that show their heads
despite our lack of interest?

Fact, act, result
-   entities that wind us with their visibility.

Time is a montage of dead bits of duration
that invent their own way to be at space
with us.

Let me portray what I am trying to say with my entire body.

I was at the clinic all day long yesterday
and being in oneself, awake to oneself

is not like throwing a ball in a dream of the world:
Think of a parabolic trajectory -
the motion of self is slow compared to that of
the hysterical egg ticking on the wall.

I wish I was covered with the agility of notions
I give to myself instead of having to wear
an oxygen mask while writing to you,
but it is the rhythmic discreetness of what I experience,
what reminds me that the hours, too, are like cysts
we can't remove: I have tried to grind their images
and eat each and every mirror that includes me,
but, as you know, the glass inside is not a frigid pile of sand
and once time has entered us, memory makes the
organs grow —as if they had no identity until now.

Space is the secondary frontier of mind
we demand from ourselves:
only dividers of our fear can adorn the place to stay.

The brain changes the matrix of empty strings
for the pillow we will die on - language.

A liturgy of encounter awaits us at the threshold
where meaning changes hands
as white carnations make room for pink.

We will discover each other at the center of no realm,
but right there where life justifies its inner laws
and determines the musicality of its forms.

Tue, May 12, 4:33 pm

Querida C,
your angelic cursive writing
dances at the top of the cliff

> where we might have merrily leapt in some pre-pubertal era.
> This was before the sanctuary was built. Peace and wisdom had search warrants slapped on them. The cliff was taller and in the place of fluorescent nooks; black tents were pitched in moonless nights.
> It was a dream back then, like now, when swaying lanterns tied to the tents hunted for your inner disciplines.

Wed, May 13, 3:42 pm

We are surrounded by the crisis of past truths:
Myths are weak like patio-table umbrellas.
Sculpting time is spitting saliva on
the circle of desires. Is there something offered
like a translucent architecture for us to recognize
a place that alters like speech ?

Night ascends to night
without retracting at all.
Names become cold models or puppets.
What is left for us under the gazebos?

We base our sense of loss upon
the obscene excess of actual.
Yet there's a tangible way to procreate
amongst others.

I am ill in every niche of existence,
the same way you are preoccupied.
Is there something missing between us?
There is a door closed between the self
and the other. We both scratch it.

It is a virtual corner
from where we exchange soundscapes,

concepts, skins as partitions of normality,
memories of what did not happen to us,
reminders of our multisensory processing.

The spectrum of spatial representation
we construct is enough for now.
Let mind represent the stitches
of a tooth extraction.

Thu, May 14, 3:58 pm

Slowing down for me is a necessity, a given
because of what I am – a living insignificance.
Clocks are violent beautifiers
winding down to our beds and oblivion is like a yellow motor.
We build maps of felt inevitability.
Pain circulates in flavorful territory
throbbing with the dread of a bird's tear
shredding it to papery bits.

Thu, May 14, 4:04 pm

Respond when time allows
increments of wellness, even if the paucity of which
stays barely above the low watermark,
to feel around your being at leisure,
whose drops I'll wait to hear.

Fri, May 15, 12:00 am

The breeze must be cold by now
in both lands of ours,
separated by an hour.
Time by man's count
signs itself on maps made by him.

We live upon those maps like toys my dear,
little toys.

I was reading Alberto Blanco when your note
swooshed in,
was reading about maps
*that are nothing but a two-dimensional representation
of a three-dimensional world
traversed by the ghost of time.*
If we can map a world of three dimensions using two,
it should be possible to map a world of four with three.

The map Columbus pursued was riddled with
geometric errors
and unaware of unseen continents,
it had brought India so close to Spain in
two-dimensions, Columbus and his men
set out for mistaken discoveries.

A holographic map should be able to map time itself.
The longest map fretted like a lattice
resides in a bird's brain.
Just as the earth never ceases to change with time, so
the history of maps never ceases to change with history
although shapes of continents change,
borders of territories and nations,
contours of rivers and mountains.

Our idea of space is a function of our idea of time
which is a landscape
we tend to draw in single dimension.
We call it Timeline.

Tue, May 26, 12:17 am

Is it possible to transform space into
a shadow-room for us to betray our figures
and take pleasure in the multiplicity of conscious life?
Things we observe are symptoms of our neurotic knowing.
Forms have blind sides
we touch like eyes that sink in their changing.
> Death is an agate in the poor horizon of experience,
> but it is the pure waiting
> in no place outside of words
> that makes everything look like history –
> in a time of our own.

Please keep writing, A
through the throbs of your beat, the history of the other sea
where silver snakes rest in the shadows of being
clustered with all of your instants, staying full of you
and full of floral youth.

The two of us are typing from the edge of
non-presence. We have no linguistic command to submerge
the heaviness of tongue. All we have is desire to name the
voluptuous subjectivity of our voices and those marks left by
objects we build.

A search for the reverse of existence
initiates on its own. We try to housetrain
our selves by disseminating
about taxonomies.
But it takes a nail to pierce a rhizome,
a series, a storage device.

If a map is nothing but a representation
of neon lights (functions),
how should we symbolize space occupied by
disease and intention?

We keep feeding from the nipple

of thought, but the traces of what we leave on
is a territory of fast deductions.

                                                        Tue, May 26, 1:58 pm

                                              Here, it's beginning to rain
                  and the forest of symbols is coming alive once again
                            those droplets on the waterlilies
                            give body to our wobbling ideas
                         about the struggle for comfort
                            of the self in its container.

                      We are feeding ourselves, both of us
                               in bodies of flesh and bone,
            in digital impressions we call letters and words
            assuming gradually, the shape of our thoughts,
            we are feeding to the uncertainties of creativity
                            and the pain of history.

                        Shall we read some Pedro Salinas
                            from his last years tonight?

Tue, May 26, 2:33 pm

A, you are a bird in the air
where the self looks for itself, where it earns for itself,
makes songs worth for what they are.
Now that the day is trapped in a lily, and that
through a motherly gesture
are born metaphors of trees and rivers,
we discover ourselves smelling like roots spread
into reality.

Thanks a great deal for inviting me to read Salinas-
his work amazes more than it moves.

Tue, May 26, 3:28 pm

What a strange landscape emerges washed with a salt rub
of loss and grief on the delectable loaf of renewal
I have found in your voice a window to awe.

Fri, Jun12, 4:21 pm

An image builds up crying atop nocturnal flowers.
I hear shredded wings and see faces drawn like small skies.
I paint the word on the sand as if it was a canvas
as if it was the word's tegument.

                                                        Fri, Jun 12, 4:38 pm

                                    Sand beats the chameleon
                 making the most dynamic of living skins
                      The sands of remembrance and loss
             upon which the best mind flourishes
                 like the stroke of an ebbing wave.
                     Are you with him? My islander?
                  graced by the uncertain goddesses
            playing alfresco in solitary anchorland
                        where he was swept in

Fri, Jun12, 4:42 pm

Here, on these ghostly streets, his alphabet moves, alongside me
following the spirit of a letter written by all the men.
       Did I see him in an impossible mirror?
Time metabolizes its own constructs.
Water strikes the day and night like a heavy soul's bell.
I find you atop the blue house

and in the desert craving like a soft stone.

Fri, Jun 12, 4:43 pm

When the image is redeployed, working and stable
it will return to that island that saved it.
Man habitually returns to his savior.
He will build a little hut there for temporary stay
bringing his harmonica and mandolin to play
to late afternoon shadows
as they sway while lengthening,
at times thinking about you.

The image of the small island
writes letters to us in strange words
which it will dispatch via sea birds.
And the same words, that evening, it will inscribe on
the sand
for the lesser goddess in the sky to read.

Fri, Jun 12, 4:47 pm

Man wakes up to a stream of weak emotions.
His islands are shaped are like playhouses
where the matrix of sound
struggles like a sparrow to convey something,
growing up as a pine
from the core of his chest.
I am listening to our voices meeting each other
with pain and elegance.

Palimpsest of the human brain reminds us
language is a screen
that allows us to see the sand while learning to cry.

Fri, Jun 19, 3:59 pm

C, we have survived
but agonize over the flowers dying near you.
Crying brings out the seas of pain, of conflict;
a desperation-vortex drilling down and
tears offering sneak previews of dead actions.

Fri, Jun 19, 4:02 pm

All life brings with it is disorders of sensation
It challenges the pattern of nerve conduction velocity
every now and then.
My leaves succumb,
branches bend beyond the breakeven
We can't smash through the odorous cortex of despair
and sleep well at the same time, but
something is progressing, I can feel, memory is progressing
as a honeycomb that houses us all.
Pain is an experience, devastation sculpts.

Fri, Jun 19, 4:04 pm

I can read your devastation.
From pain to art
is a staunching walk where no footsteps are heard,
as the shrieking shroud dampens it.
If there was something I could do
to ease that pain wriggling inside your marrow
if there was something I could do
to smear and smoothen the red squiggles
on the canvas of flesh, on the gridlock of nerves
...something.

Fri, Jun 19, 4:18 pm

There's a fragrance about your wok
a frail, sweet hint that lingers at the bottom
even after rinsing the froth away.
In the vase, the flowers have been tracked.

Where foundations lay

of forgotten bridges

Sat, Jul 4, 11:47 am

Daybreak brings on blackening activities
pulling a blanket over white preparations
of taking out and setting swan-skin filters
in the coffeemaker's brain,
and as the brewing gurgles down,
a life of sudden blackness imbues into our somnolent
selves
legumes of creative energy; black weeds
fill out in a linear disorder of terrific choice,
the white page field,
which is the new arena of study - the screen.

There, it all begins with dilemma
undertaking its ground-breaking effort
with a two-tooth hoe of desire and false belief.

Mon, Jul 13, 1:32 pm

Endearing A,
there are many holes in our theories
of cerebral functioning.
How can we remember an unintentional activity we call awakening?
Also, what do we wake up to and why?

The best evidence describing our
drifting over horizon is boredom.
Machines keep gesticulating
what we don't dare to:
the afterlives of thoughts.

We can't stop wearing black clothes
nor can we come out of our state of somnolence:
there is a knot between routines of creation.

Visual display only shows our
feet made wet by promises.

There's a sign in the trees, made as perfect as a cuckoo clock
Crying is sufficient to shape our looks at the sky
and the after-feeling of silence,
but, a land's memory can barely be measured
by the time one has spent on it.
It can be reduced to a binomial regression.

The music will reach us but where?
As if it was one's own country before ideas have come to
stay in between shadows
Shadows of the house on the road,
shadows of the sills on the house
Ashes share their tender comportment as the wind bends them
and the light of present, the birds of bearing
go to live up to the expectations of the exterior.

We drive us to an unknown bedroom
and the sun still showers us
Dying is not like flying
but growing up by the yard's kindred grass, moving constantly
until imagination washes our faces.

Tue, Jul14, 6:48 pm

Our lives burn between the limits of motion
the mind sets for us, with brief interruptions of course
of the rain pouring on the fields of flourish.
Visualize a season as an image against itself.
The heart, like a frozen gene,
is presented on a platter
in case it has learned by pure magic
something that is yet to be unearthed.

It is known how common sense warms the head

and the face beyond painted lips
beyond the cupola of longing by which we keep sowing
in the minute's garden an unseen, that we hope
will be life-like, that will be able to offer its intensities to
the present continuous.

The suffering will come. Shall we close our eyes to it?
When the simple strings of dawn hum,
will it remind us of a joy as active as silence?
Do we cry by our words?
Do we unite anywhere from our own distant countries
that will never know any more unions?
Are we like characters
that'll continue to accept the breeze of other existences?
We read the present by its perfect syllables and
resting on the poem's bed, alighting like a foolish fly
upon tongue.

                                        Thu, Jul 16, 4:54 pm

                I looked at the peachy light of this day
          across my office window and thought about …

      about the perfumed airiness of your nutty words
                 the squirrels feed on all spring,
         as branches sway from side to side stroking
               glass walls and yet stay filled
              with bushels and bushels of nuts.

             There is a subsistence farming of life
in its abandonment of established patterns and its
                  invitation of newer forms
        to simply renew, reinvigorate and regrow -
     a shifting cultivation of minds, overlaying of
                      fates and chances
        the noise in the blender coming from

> songs and cultures,
> languages and expressions,
> bodies and their sufferings.
> Does a river bring pain to its bearer
> as it sifts through cracked earth?
> This was the origin of boundary layer theory
> the life cycle of flow - from laminar to vortex
> to the death of eddies.

Sat, Jul 18, 2:02 pm

This moment without after,
this moment destined to be an easy stone
for us to walk on, is too, an interstice
from where faded tunes emanate like residual energy.
The doves try to open their eyes
They try living between us,
like waves that beat the duality of space
and brush the needy stars
Is it natural?

Harlequins dance each day
in a tiny country and the words we don´t know how to say
grow under water where the submerged hands, in vain,
search an entirety: deft hands, digits dark like that of crocs.
All moves work towards building a protection agency
for exemplary silence.
The faces suddenly light up to set us free,
to smile amongst fish.

Sat, Jul 18, 2:10 pm

Under water, like hands
stretching out to beat the barricade of coral reef
to mutual lands,
where foundations lay
of forgotten bridges,
rustier in their metallicity,
constructs meant for larger meanings ...

Sat, Jul 18, 2:12 pm

that cannot possibly be held,
built to no perfection,
standing alone, broken, incomplete,
undone like the stationary train
emptied out in the rain.
The crying train, the silencer
that arrived where it shouldn't have –
a place outside the realm and imagination of maps.

Well, what are maps really, for that matter!
Papery graphics of the unseen,
things that people fold out in the open to discover
the breadth of their desire to be outsiders.
As they say -
one is going out when a map opens out its heart
meets the light
and when it's folded back in,
learning is complete, or
the person is returning.

If the body has squeezed out like summer fruits
the pain of bearing it, sticks everywhere.

Sat, Jul 18, 2:32 pm

We come to crying with a didactic intention:
To represent some of the feelings that we experience
before the brain builds the world.
Our gestures bend distant things —seas of desire,
voices, fruits, observations.
The conflictive rhythm of sense at our fingertip,
makes us study the old products whose existence
we can't deny - tears.

Sat, Jul 18, 2:38 pm

The image has frozen its scribe.
Words won't flow after this snippet.
Let it cry.
Give it the air's silent sobs.
Tears don't just heal broken hearts
they also repair dysfunctional clocks
into which foams surf and make salt.
This wet silence, let it adjudicate.

Sat, Jul18, 2:42 pm

The findings of this study about blood pressure
and meaning circle are at our command now
But they are like pensive constellations
delaying the projection of our complaints
I wake up to your score again, dear A,
which is one landscape in itself attuned to hospitable precision.
Before the influence of your light, the will
seems to traverse like a beetle
over meadows of gratitude.

Sat, Jul 18, 2:50 pm

My islander wrote last week,
in the luminescence of the candelabrum
in his primitive cabin -
as you slept in your hospital bed,
invisible globules of scent vaporating
from your hair, face and armpit
picking up speeds greater than the engine-bird
and chose to travel to the other side of the rotary
where the lost moon was reclaimed.
While those private perfumes lingered
in a mind full of soporific sweetness,
his frivolity asked - what is usually more fretful?
the woman inside the head or the lice outside?

So much sweetness he can't handle at times,
so much unseen pain, so much crying
leaves the eyes graveled with salt-
it hurts and more tears flow
from that churning of crumbs of salt
and all sweetness turn bitter –
so much so, he wished to draw pain
as an abstract animal.

Sat, Jul18, 3:36 pm

This instant is as same as an accumulation of nights,
content with its own floods
but, I wouldn't forgive myself if my words
become the domain of obscurities standing up
against his beauty : consciousness of our condition.
It seems to be that newness can grow
between our silences like an array of street names.
We leave the sad monuments singing,
of an afternoon of perseverance
leaning over the realm of form, but the body
      breathes in its cage

and in every fallen gold leaf a controlled city is shaped.

Sun, Jul19, 1:20 am

It is the same mechanism, A
that operates in two places for you and me,
salvaging the stream of sense that works for the same sea.
Reality to this open eye,
a bell on the limits of silence.

As I think of the islander,
the sea lives twice in me
Before the thought is complete,
the exterior has been explored
It is the same pureness of yesterday's painting
that fills the ambiance of today.

Perhaps, the stone ages to rhyme with the butterflies' prayer
and behind the dreams, being burns
until it reveals its word-kernel, as if it was hidden
all this while in a perfect nest of memory
or a forest dense with the resounding signs of freedom.

Mon, Jul 20, 2:30 pm

Every grain of hemoglobin
running through your system
holds a tiny capsule of poetry,
a fluid that flushes out and via an osmosis
that love can only try to grasp
like baby fingers, my dear,
reaching for the glass on the table
a newness, a *quelque choze* called glass.

Tue, Jul 21, 7:42 pm

I speak to the islanders of this day, search for their voices,
want to describe their pelican-like heads
It is an accidental gesture that keeps the search going
for the heart of man,
the zeal for writing about the realms life creates for us,
its quotidian offer along with its numerous forbidden moons
and treacherous songs.
Eyes move together,
as if they were baptizing themselves
before something excessive
Which redundant force does time talk to us about?
What ray does life act by when the peripheral self burns?

Tue, Jul 21, 7:46 pm

Senses are apparatus with gages on their outside
that are meant to assess and measure
what we live amongst and experience;
but as the appraisal grows, we learn to recreate
land and skyscapes that describe ourselves,
personal requiems to coronate loss;
loss of shapes, for example, in the shadows of roses.

Tue, Jul 21, 8:08 pm

There are some species of fish whose voluptuous shapes
expose us to the profiles of our own personality.
If the sea is alive, what grows up against it?
Before memory's allegiance to the stars fade,
we imagine the earth as a bedroom within another.

The pulp torments,

inside unspent juices churn

Thu, Jul 30, 5:11 pm

Dear A, we have tried to press the egg of silence,
that excrescence of continuity
protected by the world:
Mouths are the owners of their shadows
and exhale the vapor of false orchards.
Let us only listen to visceral songs.
It is a collection of little dolls
we are given upon
a fabric of strict nouns.
Whether we devour dead skin
or change desires,
the kingdom of sensation is always incomplete:
Time has grains rising up to the daily sun.

We are one with nature. There is nowhere to go but
surfaces around the hive of activity-
a single cell of the comb of present.
Fate shows like recent grass we are interested in.
We can take to cleansing flights
during spells of transitioning weather.

Wasps urinate on our tents

Thu, Jul 30, 5:38 pm

And the throbbing gulls?
They remind of the circulation of words
that flesh out language, which becomes ourselves
drawing closer by the day
as if the sea was a can of nihility
membrane of welkin
separating celestial bodies

Thu, Jul 30, 6:07 pm

Time bears within itself
marks of circulation left by us,
commotion that helps us
elongate the tenuous passages from
habits to acts of transcendence.
Pleasure brings with it
samples of pale yellow starks men have wiggled in,
bearing proof of beings in disguise.

Thorns of totality
remind us that voices wither as any other
object of mind and knots of senses
show us nothing but the impact of thirst.

            Fri, Jul 31, 6:54 pm

              Voices stay alive
      to send homing pigeons to each other
    providing flesh to the time feathering them.
       Ears raise, the vein in the throat
         feels vibes, infrasounds heard
     and how hands come over one another
            one cannot see.
     We read to each other in the tree-house
       and the sky kept coughing around
           to tell its presence.

Fri, Jul 31, 7:04 pm

It is the medium of propagation
of shapes, the amputated light from reality
which serves as a source of our returns.
We pass from doubt to doubt, feeling
the squeeze among grapes, because
what ignited the being once,

that seed is pressed by ants,
that lack of contradiction
building itself in accordance with the track
of novelty, is not separated
from the moss colony of memory.

We live in need of a hierarchy of ambiances
but the absorption of moments
spent with others by devices of representation
doesn't harden without repetition:
the absent is meant to stay inside, in multiplicity and
self-sufficiency, just like the water
we look across from the tree-house
and the swallows in blindness.

Fri, Jul 31, 8:08 pm

We work on the center buffer coupling all day
at the join of the first and second signal systems
where the weight of digital ether
comes down on the amorphous unborn
with gushing steam;
to forge words, cog and sprocket them
into a roll of bogies -
phrases, expressions,
finally a sentence
mediating between stasis and turbulence

Fri, Jul 31, 8:36 pm

Acts of volition
don't negate the monotonous landscape of our wanting
Tongue prospers by a motion of larva
from heavy circuits of thought
to the austere atmosphere of speech,
there is nothing but a web of life.

It is a system of reverberation that
shines in the mirror of dream.
When felt past finds exit,
it is hope that makes us sculpt
what it knows about ourselves.

The pain of being in time
can't be consumed like hay
The hours make us linger in their commodities
Nothing at all seems to raise
from the exterior of possibility–
without a room for the sensual
no metabolic deviation from oblivion is easy.

Chance incentives the afternoon in all of us
We are given a feather, a dust cloud,
a created predicament to be placed in relation with
imagination.

Yet we will never know the maximum value of
waiting. The inside is measured by failures.
Men can never perform the elegies of childhood
far from home.

However, touching is to set free
our spectral strings in a tender horizon.

Fri, Jul 31, 8:44 pm

There is somewhere around each one of us C
that infinity sign, that analemma.
Our petals sprout at the very center of that shape
at an intersection, a point of double inflexion.

Seeing things round and round
do not remind me of the circle, in geometric purity
A vortex instead, lurching the will to survive forward
with fate's occasional backward pull

- a spring action of sorts in a viscous medium
alternating progression and regression
as the snake moves
and the rose swirls in and out
living on and on
as long as the world needs it.

Fri, Jul 31, 8:58 pm

We lick the salt of wish in consternation.
It is uncertainty that interferes with
our discourses and activities.
All of us are given a residue of force
to build a bridge bearing in it
our ways of being and our prophecies.
We shepherd dichotomies
from one page to another.
There are correspondences in
our domain of lightness
we see as offerings –
the looking-glass of breath
containing relationships with the infinite elements
of flagellates.

Anything left behind by others -its invented beauty or ugliness
will complete us in its own way.
Poetry owns the big wing of feeling, of fate
stitches verbs and while weathering the hours
structures our response to
the changes of skin.

Mon, Aug 3, 3:45 pm

It showed
after they all left -
colorful skeletons
shards of dead butterflies

It showed
tumorously suspended from the lines -
near empty now as they
mostly left, notes of hung discord
on a chromatic scale

It showed
what had flung far in sonorous absences
That speck of luster amongst
the henbit below

It showed
the origin of misheard tunes of the months
and how unmistakably it had chimed
with their foregone winds

Slept with lightning striking the dark contours
of the blue spruce next to my window
woke up with the same shiver
I had submitted to last night
as if I had slept for a wink.

Thu, Aug 13, 3:18 pm

My islander,
he was recently enchanted by a birdcall
from a species unknown so much so
he urged the governess of poetry to switch him with it.

With exchanged identities
he now can fly to trees near you
and perch on them as a solar colleague
wishing to watch you shed your silken petals
in lunar incense.

Thu, Aug 13, 4:31 pm

Something sticks to our throats:
The agent determining longevity of knowledge.
The worm that pierces
the core of the self- the ephemeral bond we create
with ourselves.

We sleep where the exemplary veil of summer falls.

There are alphabets
explosive and orphaned like winds
that are able to make orchids float in nostalgic ecstasy.

Thu, Aug 13, 4:35 pm

There are also
scores of rivers and millions of trees
displacing air shafts between our rooms.
Rooms that have switched places.
Rooms that exchange programs allocated to us;
your room locates you
like phones locate people these days
and yet you barely know the poignancy
of its climate; you barely know the occupant
how he lives and works in there by the hour.

Thu, Aug 13, 4:46 pm

Conscious melancholy
begins with an erection of language.
The milk of meaning leaves the body
through the presence where it cracked.
We feel the world in erosion.

Thu, Aug 13, 7:17 pm

Man's face is always surrounded by smoke,
with the smear of recent ash, like a seal
ashes of the states of will.
Ways of beauty get lost in the effects of rain.
We forget about the preludes of hope
as death calls:
nothing taller than death itself, just the separation.
Separation of powers of self, of body and mind
driven by negative procedure.

The word is pregnant with the purest fruits of loss.
Memory grows by virtue of violent translations,
of patterns of saturation.
Anything felt in time and space becomes
the ground for an olive tree just outside your room
and someone who sat on its branch
with legs dangling, still belongs to us.

Fri, Aug 14, 5:08 pm

At times you and your room are removed
like the black box and its algorithm.
Agents of flowers work away from them
in the air, through the wind.

And my room is just the same -
bemused, entrenched within you
where the reductionist image magnifies
until it is real life again
seated on the corner sofa with
untied hair curling to the right of
your face like black sea-froth,
the image wore an ocean night-sky
crusted with navy blue leaves

upon which icicles hanging from all dead, cold stars
dripped a dew you cried
from each sordid night of the heart.

Our rooms contain ourselves
and themselves
Our rooms are built inside each other.

Fri, Aug 14, 5:38 pm

Dearest A,
where we assume the shape of autumn leaves
and that of a tube full of noble gas,
where we become opportunities of self-reflection
confronting them at the intervals of madness,
but if our rooms wither in the wait for ourselves,
what will rise from its ruins ?

Perhaps a perfume that invades us
and the rooms we built,
that of people passing from the monologues of desire
to monologues of pain.

Asterisk of sadness
can draw our bodies near a hollow filled with red spiders:
going beyond the way we discover
who we are and aren't in our distant worlds.

We sing, disciplined, amongst the mountains of impatience.
Languages share moments that won't become anything
but mills of aesthetic illusion.
Words are liquid eyes searching for new dimensions.

                                              Fri, Aug 14, 7:18 pm

                                            They are like shoes, C
                                that ambition to walk the complete beach
                                                   get weary, sleep and
                                        get run-over like the F... O'Hara
                                                        darling O'Hara.

                                                 It takes time dearest,
                                                    the growth of the spirit
                                takes efforts of plastering, building layers
                                             until a flight of stairs figure
                              we climb up to a state of a wider pause -
                                                    the landing of desire

Fri, Aug 14, 7:25 pm

But before that arrives, we get to know
the burning segment first and then move on
to the other figures of experience.
They offer their joy of the mute sun, defend natural landscape.
The redundancies of sound make us feel stronger.
But the wine tasted in stillness keeps us convinced:
life is a small cup of whole milk
and desire, its invisible froth.

Wed, Sep 9, 10:55 pm

Presence allows for monotonous structures,
scores similar to the sight of swans on a lake in winter.
Flowers open up to successive states of form.
Things created in exchange are part of a performance
reserved in the spaces where the mind can recover from
its poverty of sensations,

where the unimportant seem to churn away from us,
where there is a wand of young light waving over debris:
a maze of scar tissues.

Wed, Sep 9, 11:54 pm

Of the many degrees of freedom
manifesting in a swan, one is lost as a feather
suspended from the hilltop, overlooking ancient
translucence structured like a city.

As a symbol of freedom it culls brittle evanescence,
managing to compress itself into a thin layer
held tight between approaching faces that remain
separated so as to dispel love –
love reified as freedom,
but weighing down hearts held in rusty cupolas
in the cold, pressurized bottoms of green seas.

Freedom self-reflects as a plant without a stalk,
that has come off a larger assembly –
an integral of whose holistic freedom it was a part –
an emblem of you
at the center of your rising nipple.

Thu, Sep 10, 12:01 am

Unity of dual
mediates on sequences of solitude.
It is hard now, not to slow down the spectacle of encounters
when the apple peels roast in the heat of freedom,
freedom of dream, of language.

Though that oneself, remains chastely sane
while being in the throes of total fire
is a triumph of will.

All moments of possibility burn more than us:
some of them become
marigold petals and mud pellets, secret subtlety inherited.

Thu, Sep 10, 12:03 am

Pain imposes its own self upon body
It makes its essence circulate through
organs and apparatus.
Tongues of birds have a wide variety of
shapes and features.
I know mine is like a dusty box where
my song distempers.

The pulp torments, inside unspent juices churn.

I think of rejected waves. Think about sacrifices
beyond this cage.
The vase holds an image of the being -
I am in need of existing, of becoming someone else.
Uncertainty has been just a little too hard on me.
Perhaps I am portraying my prejudices and fears.
I'm not a castaway, but I live on the edge of self.

Human voice projects itself
on the ideal stream of conscious activities.
In my bedroom upstairs from where every opinion
appears cloudy, at times, the rhythm of spring
fails to reach us,
but never mind dear,
failure doesn't work except in defense of beauty.

Thu, Sep 10, 12:29 am

I have been listening to myself for hours.
My throat feels pierced, full with the extravagance

of needlessness, the anti-gravity of big kites.
The genealogy of ideas is as frail as this
winter light. Reason is the knife dividing
our modes of pure existence
the tumors in our eyes and lips.

Fri, Sep 11, 6:54 am

Things extraneous to the body will eventually find one
According to the lemma, all of the distempered purple
lacquer pours into an ink pot at the horizon.
The remaining hues, hinting at fall,
explain a pigmentation problem
that's short and summarized.
Reflecting on the situation does not transmit it
but puts a mirror between us as you have observed,
doubling the suffering.
But there is a communion near the sky-bridge
which smuggles the devil across.
My pistol sparkles and as syncope spares you,
sweet center,
we figure its loss of raw mass and meat
turn into a conversation about withering.

Fri, Sep 11, 9:09 pm

It is not absurd to think that
consciousness is made of voracious simulations,
of cups of denial. There is always a threshold
of emotions we try to modify, a railway crossing
of validity
our right to live
to feel
to reflect
and pass through.

Fri, Sep 11, 7:50 pm

I think of a simulacrum too, of life
modeled after a master pattern
transformed into the real space of the personal
following not algorithms of nature so much,
like certain petals follow Fibbonacci sequence,
but by inequalities of multiple inheritances,
each one a new method, a variation
of a discovered law of probability,
many of which the birds know better than us
laws that penguins learn from ice;
laced by principles and structures of destruction
this simulacrum dwells within a delicate matrix
of vulnerability.

Fri, Sep 11, 8:59 pm

We all are allowed thoughts about an absence of being.
There are always clouds segregating interior islands
from rings of silence.

I have been listening to myself for years.
A maze of dead tissue has grown like submarine algae
under the influence of my voices.
No star shows because I salivate
I know the rachitic balance of my gesture
The rain doesn't. Yet the rain is not an easy wine either
sniffing at my organism with a jealousy
My body smells almost like a metabody
between body states.

If reality became a honeybee
sucking shapes assumed by our knowledge of it,
words we use to name forms of misery we reproduce and
massive superstitions we adopt, are nothing but
noble shoes we carry on our head.

It is pain, dear A, that is at the center of my created world.
I can't forget ruptures of wish,
the noisy objects of beauty moving to disappear
in unseen sand.

Life continues to be a dress with floral designs
made with black lines, intense ascendants
That was a different rain I told you about sometime back
and the purple umbrella
under which I walked as a teenager
into the dripping woods.

Sat, Sep 12, 7:22 pm

DO NOT ENTER

please, do not.

black cats and digitized omens.
The alley is dark
but all automobiles can be parked on all sides

What is crisscrossing outside the window
is flaky and shredded
If I say cotton balls
it's the dark chapter speaking with
a suppression of the baleful -
letters from prison, censored lines struck through
in dense black bold

lengthy Proustian sentences with a few fluttering
punctuations - that's the gulls
in near empty panorama - still life on the waves
pixels everywhere with a consternation of flickering
but out of it things jump - kites, fish

                    Jack is dead in the box
               and pain returns unnoticed
       in a small group of caterpillars working
                      on the laces of her bed
                        waiting to greet death
               with new birth-shots of color

                                The alley is dark
                                       and open

Sat, Sep12, 11:33 pm

I remember that night
It is the night we return to:
Mind keeps reverberating
because of inertias of understanding.
One has to bear the nausea of birth
the clock on the table.

I walk inside seeing ourselves stretch
arms to enter the hole-rooms of meaning.
I walk inside listening to you.

Memory now lives beyond the field where
the sparrows used to pee,
within the limits of songs.

Talking about limits -
words, for me, are islands of anxiety
with their deltas forming
of froth and foam,
salt and sand,
in the drift of my crumbling imagination.

I'm an assembly of nervous winds
and I know the most tempting benefits
of agitation, but
If I think about the real frontiers of innocence

if I think about the measure of things
body and shadow are the same:
made of the pure ingredients of pain and life.

I´m learning to use identity
as objects of cognition
that don't deny their obedience
to the iridescent aura of emptiness
to the wind vanes.

Wed, Dec 2, 9:49 am

Today, my effort to join two hands,
and believe in myself, the mutual poverty
of two bodies that summon each other to believe
in themselves. With joined hands,
rather than mourning the colors that did not
last in flesh, I would like to keep,
in the pocket of a moment
one whole word the sun can't deny.

Even the void is available to touch
by means of a virtual striptease of verbs
We take our clothes off not looking for nudity
but a continuum of cells - body within body
Everything else is the transforming of being
into an erection of itself. We rub them
Rub our bodies of expression upon another
Could you come deep inside me now?
As deeply as possible?

Wed, Dec 2, 8:07 pm

I come in as hands inside wet, luscious earth
hands full of seeds, that have dual purpose –
to plow but also to feel
intended action, unknowingly pushing

the membranes of the implied

Wed, Dec 2, 9:36 pm

It is not always the perception of boundaries
but the fluid infrastructure of selves
where we intercept and unite.
What would it be like to live without a language
that produces luring objects and ideas?
We both know the velocity of sound
by the motion of a tongue that reflects on another.
At times, it is the visceral connection
between the lines we write that narrates this becoming
of us as a colorful flux of voices.
Brain connects the depilated doors, but it is by squeezing
the bells and showering us with their juices
that we become the flow of desire.

Wed, Dec 2, 10:01 pm

The theory of miscibility,
whether it applies to language or our bodies,
is about the struggle of flowstreams to adjust
to their needs, forming eddies and vortices
in the wake of imaginary sea creatures
always leaving gaps, voids, pockets of turbulence
like wounds....
Desire is the wound of reality

As osmosis demonstrates

this invisible dye of pain

Dec 5 – Dec 31

We know that we are
surrounded by the bustle of life
that gives shape to sand everyday.
Years and years spent to feel the form
of a plastic bag,
the sun dead among words, the latencies of the self.
No consolidation of memory is
the interruption of absence of ourselves
which is not to say there is no memory but that
of a void; there are symbols and residue everywhere -
the confetti of existential cycles spread all around and
beyond us, preserved for the sake of its strangeness.
All recollections and reflections of reality
have the consistency of the chain links of language,
forming an array of schooners.
It is difficult for us to come to terms with
the direction of life inside life
the form of bodies inside the body
the magic car can't completely control its driver
the tree can't catalyze season
This minute is not a picture frame of everyone's time and space
yet we can't seem to live out of the state of mind it dictates.
No realm is forever. Not even the ideas.

Many times I've wondered,
as now, if in their idle friction
and humble happiness,
the minutes, which today
have a heart of their own,
and have left the clock in the
hands of the handless
flying to the unseen controllers
of hot-air balloons, only
to return flaccid in secondary
eddies to force us to see what
we are not anymore, to force

us to look at who we were
while taking the lie detector test or
as tight rope unicyclists masked as harlequins
trying to run against time,
against everything that lives
longer than ourselves.

In and out of the present moments,
some of us, seem gone
like daffodils, a little later like tulips
like gumballs in the dispenser
but today, it allows us to
feel the furious correspondence
of the infinite world of meaning at the edge of our
floral blue shower curtain
twined with our intimate
and convalescent allure.
Would it be the same without having lost a bit
of that fulminant delectation?
Would it be the same dying without having treasured
a bit of that static pulsation?
But as you know, because color flows
it has a body and limbs and can travel
from a source of higher concentration
to a lesser, if we could build bridges across
cups to share some coffee.

Or, like a raisin shriveled
in the sweetness of pain, submerged in a glass
of water - life becomes obedient to its invisible
laws. The voice lives on without itself
in a drift of sensations.

Many times I've wondered,
as now, how does it grow - that
ambiguous nipple against everything

deserted? How, as osmosis demonstrates
this invisible dye of pain infiltrating the lesser body,
as it embraces the shriveled. How do the lips
tolerate silence or a wounded word?
if today's song of innocence swerves
like a dream carved on a sleeping body,
like a dream carved without time,
where the blood is proud.

But, wondering is still feeling,
and feeling is still knowing
that the minutes count to
keep pace and rhythm in the inside of the organ -
the inset of clock-tick.

Mirror against mirror, image against image,
shadow against shadow, mind fails us
and builds fractals around ourselves
that get viral like fern.
We know how to separate ourselves
from chapter endings, as waves separate from waves
like things felt in time dissever
from our sources to belong to their kernels of truth.

Talking is still thinking
and thinking is still feeling
life as one whole, a disjointed whole
but conjoined still with the system that
holds it, the pan-handle
of loss that holds us all.

The kernel is not just where life began,
it has a life of its own. A recurrence
to which the minutes count.

The thresholds count as proof of the
pain that lives within us like an unborn.
Pain counts to the heart and looking at myself is
still knowing and feeling that
I´m am being displaced from the image of my body,
but not from pain, because the kernel controls.
It is that center, the infallible, scientific center
which controls all labor in an uncontrollable desire
to grow. And just as I work hard to manage pain
we all do, work hard and harder from day to day
with ardor, zeal, élan and with so much industriousness
that the industry collapses.

Perhaps, in just a minute,
returning with irresistible youth
and its imagined reserve,
it is enough to be on the
earth without being oneself.

Will those moments I spent with myself return
to force me to look at the distortion
in the mirror today?
The look of a beingless naked?
Time, doesn't push its threshold
of suffering and as always, I wonder whether
the earthy minutes make perfect
my substance, my presence.
I wonder if they let me choose
a certain look.

After all we are bodies and
transmigration needs to crack my inside up
in order to travel, even in the entrails of our
long, wide globally warming hug.
You can hear feelings but not these
silent crackles old mirrors envy.

Is it therefore like the way
we announce our plans and positions
in words unspoken?
Doesn't it feel like a little pain that is
packed inside so many of us
that time seems to pass by
without touching?
Subsumed in a leafy fruit bowl
our organic questions decay
from lack of human touch.

Sometimes, like today, I wonder
whether such earthy minutes
have perfected my substance.
Today, when pain counts to
the heart, I feel the
the images of the toughest
clocks are themselves,
like an excess of life, which
we still need to know, to which
we still need to stay exposed.

Life doesn't have to rest.
As autumn eats dead time
lizards pierce the fruits of sleep.
How the minutes manage to live
under our feet is in question, but robbed of time,
the seed in my chest continues to dream
and the chosen periphery of things
that throb like words, cramps too.
We keep no secret to ourselves
seeds whisper to the earth to bring on new skin
that dreams of the next bodyform,
as the next minute is dreamed
and when the shape is assumed
no one flips the hourglass.

Cristina Sánchez López is a counselor, sociologist and bilingual poet from Medellin, Colombia. Her poems have appeared in numerous literary magazines, such as La Jiribilla, Diario Gráfico de Xalapa (Veracruz, Mexico), Urcunina literary magazines (Colombia), Los Escribas (Mexico), The MUD Proposal and Kaurab (Kolkata, India). Anthology appearances include A Mar Abierto (To Open Sea, SEPIA Edi-ciones, Mexico, 2014) and latin american poetry anthology Esta ternura y estas manos libres (This tenderness and these free hands, Editorial Touchstone, Colombia, 2015). She is working on three poetry manuscripts - "Archaeology of Autumn", "Songs for fall", "Symphony of abandonment".

Aryanil Mukherjee is a bilingual Asian American writer who has authored fourteen books of poetry, essays and fiction in two languages and a book of poems in Spanish translation from Amargord, Spain. Engaged in bi-directional translation of poetry between English and Bangla Aryanil has translated scores of international poets including a book-length translation project on John Ashbery. Aryanil edits KAURAB (http://www.kaurab.com), a celebrated avant-garde Bengali literary magazine in print since 1970 and on the web since 1998. He works as an engineering mathematician in Cincinnati, Ohio.